T0208801

Endorsements

"The mind of a golfer is a complex one. Simply doing as Bill states, will unclutter the mind of the perplexed golfer and reinforce that there is no longer walk in golf than the one from the practice tee to the first tee. I have been witness to Bill's countless hours of research and development, and the end result is quite entertaining."

Travis Mann, General Manager & Executive Professional, Granite Pointe Golf Club, Nelson, BC

"In this book Bill has captured the struggle every golfer faces as they try to master the concepts of the game without being overwhelmed by the complexities that confuse us all. This look at some very simplistic advice will be a stroke saver for most golfers, especially the 90 plus player."

Brian DeBiasio, Former Canadian Mid-Amateur Champion

"I don't golf but I think Bill gives good advice, especially in Chapter 4 about the long irons. Actually, the advice about the small stuff is good too in Chapter 11."

Bill's sister, Heather

Golf Solved

Also by Bill Reid

101 Nifty Ideas for High Schools

A Baby Boomer's Guide to "I Remember When . . ."

G●lf Solved

A Tongue-In-Cheek Guide to Simply Doing the
Obviously Simple to Improve Your Golf Game

Bill Reid

 iUniverse®

Golf Solved
A Tongue-In-Cheek Guide to Simply Doing the
Obviously Simple to Improve Your Golf Game

iUniverse books may be ordered through booksellers or by contacting:

iUniverse
1663 Liberty Drive
Bloomington, IN 47403
www.iuniverse.com
1-800-Authors (1-800-288-4677)

ISBN: 978-1-4502-5309-3 (sc)
ISBN: 978-1-4502-4208-0 (e)

Print information available on the last page.

iUniverse rev. date: 11/20/2017

With thanks to the Thursday night golfing partners at Granite Pointe Golf Club who provided the inspiration to put these pithy thoughts in writing and offered advice on my draft copy

Frank Arabia
Paul Belanger
Alan Burch
Gary Schmidt
Dean Studer
Howie Ridge
Larry Tremblay
Larry Veregin

On the Cover

Looking out over Kootenay Lake towards
the Kokanee Glacier from the 16th tee box
at Granite Pointe Golf Course
in Nelson, British Columbia

Golf is a game, any way you slice it

Table of Contents

Appendices

List of Illustrations

Introduction

I've been golfing for quite a few years and have supported the golf ball retail industry in a prolific way, supported it to the degree that I see Wal Mart selling recycled used golf balls. Recycled, used golf balls! Can you imagine? So many lost golf balls in this world that huge department store chains have product availability to maintain an inventory. And what a windfall for governments! Sales tax on a product that gets sold over and over again.

The only way to avoid supporting this incredible industry is to improve your skill level to the point where you improve your score and don't lose balls. If you do not lose golf balls, your score will improve. There is a direct, statistical correlation between lost golf balls and scores. It sounds easy, but it is not. And the game itself so insidiously creeps into the human psyche that you cannot do the most obvious thing to stop the losses, you cannot stop playing.

If you must play, there is only one alternative. You have to improve your game. You have to finish your round of golf with the same ball you started with. That most surely sounds simple, but, not surprisingly, it is not. IT IS NOT!!

Now I golf every Thursday at Granite Pointe Golf Club, the local course in Nelson, in the Men's Night competition. Eighteen holes of golf and 2 or 3 cans of beer (I say 2 or 3 because to say otherwise might suggest that alcohol is a factor in the loss of golf balls, and we cannot allow that thought). I am fortunate in the friends with whom I golf. Decent people, people who care about the game, students of the game, assiduous promoters of the sport, and people who wish to improve. This book salutes their many suggestions and ideas.

It is constructive criticism, calmly suggested, ruefully pondered, sometimes dryly proposed and at the heart of it is the simple nugget of truth which, if considered and acted upon, would most definitely have resulted in a better shot. It is also the suggestion of someone who has just seen the error and with that incredible hindsight, which allows all golfers to be experts even of those who toil on the professional circuit, the spoken suggestion is so obviously correct that one can do little but self-berating for not thinking of it before the shot.

So, dear reader and golf aficionado, you no doubt have this fine book in your hands because you too wish to benefit from the wisdom of my friends, because you too wish to lose fewer golf balls, and because you too wish to improve your game. We can do all three.

And this I can guarantee you, that if you see the mistakes you have been making in these pages and follow the suggested corrections, you will take many strokes off your score.

It's just that simple.

Chapter One:

Putting

Some golfers say that you drive for show and putt for dough. In other words, the short putt is a stroke that counts as much as the longest drive. So, it is important to make those putts go into the hole. There are many common mistakes and in the pages to follow, I review each mistake and show the simple correction required. I also include a Super-Hint, a single hint that will take your game to a much higher level altogether. And for your convenience, all Super-Hints are collated at the end of the book as Appendix D. Print out that single page and take it with you whenever you golf.

So let's get started.

If you find that your putts are not reaching the hole, as illustrated in Figure 1, you will never have a good score. The fix is easy and is given below the illustration.

Figure 1: Putt not Reaching the Hole

A very frustrating miss which can be easily avoided by hitting the ball harder so that it actually reaches the hole and preferably has enough power to go past the hole if the hole is missed. Try it and see for yourself. Before you leave the green, replace your ball and hit the putt again, but this time, hit it harder. See? It does work. And note for the file: if you are putting uphill, you will have to hit harder than if you are putting downhill. Pay attention to this as it is more important than the direction of the grain of the grass (unless you are playing on Bermuda).

If you find that your putts are going past the hole, you have the opposite problem illustrated in Figure 2. However, it is complicated by the fact that, if you are beyond the hole, you hit too hard and with poor direction. The poor direction is the subject of later hints. In terms of hitting past the hole, the correction follows the illustration.

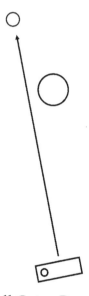

Figure 2: Ball Going Beyond the Hole

To remedy this unfortunate but common error, hit the ball more lightly. A slower putter-head speed through impact will result in the ball travelling less distance.

If you find that your putts are going left as illustrated in Figure 3, there is a simple solution.

Figure 3: Putt Going Left

A very frustrating miss which can be easily avoided by aiming more to the right. Try it and see for yourself. If you miss by 4 inches (approximately 9 cm), then aim 4 inches to the right next time and enjoy the feeling of seeing that putt drop straight down into the cup.

If you find that your putts are going right as illustrated in Figure 4, you have the opposite problem of Figure 3 and the solution is the opposite too, assuming of course that your vision is good and you have not forgotten your glasses or contacts at home if you wear them.

Figure 4: Putt Going Right

As is clear from the illustration, the remedy is to aim more to the left. However, do not let concentration on the aim result in a loss of focus on the speed of the putt, otherwise we bring Figures 1 and 2 into play again possibly resulting in what is technically called a "five putt," too long, too short, to the left, to the right, and into the hole. Five strokes within six feet. Sheesh, no wonder putting is for the dough. Note that with some playing partners, a four-putt means buying a jug of beer in the clubhouse, so extra diligence is called for after two putts without even thinking about five.

If you find that your putts are going off the green, either you are on a severe downhill lie or your perception of distance is suspect. The severe downhill lie is an acceptable excuse in most groups, but the poor perception of distance is generally considered laughable and is best avoided by greater concentration or less alcohol on the course.

The Putting Super-Hint

Chip the ball into the hole from off the green. Never take your putter out of the bag. The advantages are incredible and include a huge reduction in putts per round, a dramatically lower score per hole, and irreplaceable savings in equipment as you can buy a cheap used putter at a garage sale with a nice putter-head cover so that it looks expensive.

Please see Appendix A for the Putting Tracker Grid which can be torn from the book and which will record your putting tendencies, thus allowing you to concentrate on problem areas using the advice offered in the putting chapter.

Chapter Two:

Chipping

A good chipping game is fundamental to lower scores. This is especially true for those who experience some or all of the putting flaws described in Chapter One. A well placed chip which results in the ball being within a club length of the hole is a tremendous boost to having a good game.

Chipping is generally used to get the ball from off the green to near the hole. It may require flying the ball over water or a bunker to reach the flag. Chipping out of longer grass near the green is not uncommon. Most golfers use a wedge to chip but all other clubs may be called into play depending upon the exact situation. On rare occasions you may see a player chipping with a driver, but great care is required as it can easily lead to the situation where you never get on the green.

Common mistakes and their remedies are in the pages to follow. The common mistakes are topping the ball, hitting too high or low and hitting too far or not far enough.

Considering that there are entire golf schools built around the short game, it is quite evident that following the advice which follows is a money-saving way to make golf more enjoyable.

If you find that the chipped ball goes nowhere or does not get into the air, you will not be the first amateur golfer to suffer this indignity. Observe in Figure 5 how the tip of the blade of the club brushes across the extreme upper edge of the ball. This ball will never become airborne. The correction is one of the simpler ones

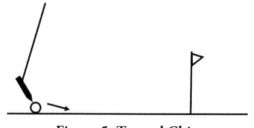

Figure 5: Topped Chip

Do not hit the top of the ball with your club. You need to hit under the ball, to get it into the air. Start back slowly and accelerate through the ball with a crisp smooth motion. The ball will lift nicely. Ensure that you have aimed the ball towards the hole before initiating the accelerating motion.

The chip shot may sometimes go really high in the air and then come back down just a few feet in front of you. This is caused by a highly lofted club sliding under the ball. Be less concerned about this error as it can sometimes be seen on television in a professional tournament as even the professionals will sometimes get "under" the ball if the grass is high.

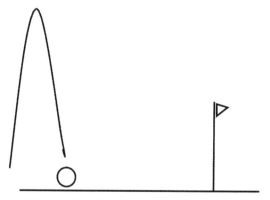

Figure 6: Chip too high in the Air

There are a couple of solutions to this problem. Simplest is to take better practice swings to achieve the correct place to hit the ball and then hit the ball correctly. Another possibility is to use a club with less "loft" so that you have more surface to connect with the ball. Be careful not to hit the ball in its "equator" with the pitching wedge as you may see a ball that was supposed to go only 40 feet travel well over 100 yards. This could negatively affect your score.

If you find your chips are consistently landing in water or sand, there are two possibilities. One possibility is that you are not reaching the green and the other, more frustrating, is that you are going too far. If you do both on the one hole, people will shake their heads at you. Don't let that happen. Follow the instruction below.

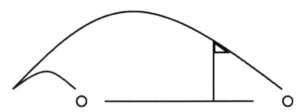

Figure 7: Chip Short into Water/Sand or Long into Water/Sand

Either you have to hit the ball harder (if the water/sand is on the near side) or more lightly (if the water/sand is on the far side of the green)

One would think that a chip shot, which is played relatively close to the green, would have a reasonable chance of going directly towards the flag. Alas, golf is not always a reasonable game and you may find the chip shot ending up left of the pin. This problem is illustrated in Figure 8 and the problem resolved below.

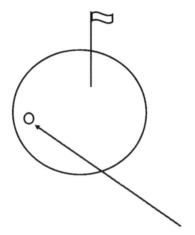

Figure 8: Chip goes to the Left

As the illustration demonstrates, this chip has ended up about 20 feet left of the hole. The correction is to hit the ball more to the right, aiming directly towards the hole or just slightly left or right as determined by the slope of the green which I know you were smart enough to already take into account. Aim less to the left to improve your score.

The other common miss with the chip shot, not surprisingly, is to hit the ball too far to the right as illustrated in Figure 9.

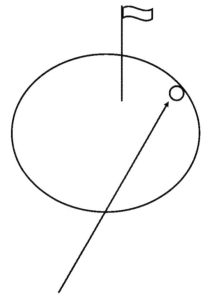

Figure 9: Chip Goes to the Right

Once again, a frustrating miss resulting in a longer putt than would be necessary had the chip been hit more directly towards the flag (and the correct distance). A proper chip would have been aimed more to the left, bringing the hole into play. Make the appropriate adjustment the next time you face this shot by choosing an appropriate target zone located on the green and based upon the slope.

Another important factor in chipping in some groups is the generosity of the playing partners. Surely "within the leather" of the putter handle is close enough to the hole (belly putters excepted).

The Chipping Super Hint

Hit the green with your fairway woods. Eliminate the need to chip. You will not need to carry three wedges in your bag, making everything lighter and the bag easier to carry. You also avoid worrying about the distance that each club, with its loft, will carry the ball with a full swing, half swing, quarter swing, etc. You can also stop worrying about the amount of "bounce" there is on the bottom of the club and focus more clearly on whether or not it has a grip you like.

Please see Appendix B for the Chipping Tracker Grid which is designed to allow you to identify your tendencies while chipping and make the correct remediation and thereby lower your score.

Chapter Three:

On the Tee Hitting the Driver

As mentioned in Chapter One, you drive for show and putt for dough. However, there is no greater feeling (other than an extremely long putt dropping into the hole) than solid connection between the driver and the ball resulting in the ball briskly leaving the tee with a comforting, solid, clicking sound and a furious flight forward and straight for hundreds of yards ending with a soft, satisfying draw or gentle fade into the centre of the fairway, a shot that allows you to utilize the chipping super hint and score a quick eagle on a par 4, one of the most pleasing aspects of the game. The long drive also results in copious "oooohs" and "ahhhhs" from your playing partners, sometimes to the point where you swing even more mightily on your next shot to go even further, and end up suffering a missed shot

Alas, with great distance available, great variations in flight path come into play and can result in some terrible outcomes with your driver. If they do, and I say "if" because for me the glass is half full and you likely will make a decent shot, if they do, please pay close attention to the tips in this chapter to make the driver in your bag the powerful club that it so wishes to be.

Let's get started. If you take a mighty swing and miss the ball, you will find that the first tip will set you straight and give you the necessary confidence. The flaw and correction are in Figure 10

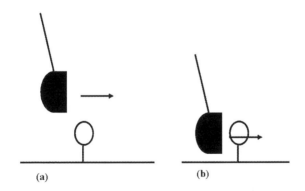

(a)   (b)

Figure 10: Driver Misses the Ball

Figure 10 (a) clearly shows that if you swing above the ball, there is no possible way to make the ball go straight and long, and in fact, not even straight. While some may think the correction is to use a higher tee, this would be a poor solution for several reasons. One, eight inch tees are bulky and not readily available in good golf outlets. Two, an unusually high tee will make your friends laugh at you. Three, a very high tee most often results in another difficult problem in which the club head passes under the ball and as an outcome, the tee is broken and the ball merely drops a few inches straight down costing you a stroke and inability to re-tee the ball as you must (should) play it where it lies.

No, the proper correction is to hit the ball with the centre of the club head striking the centre of the ball as the club head commences its upwards motion in its flight arc as shown in Figure 10 (b).

A great challenge with the driver is hitting the fairway. Even the professionals face this challenge. The difference between landing on the fairway and landing left or right of it can be the difference between a record setting personal best and a dismal, we-can-throw-away-this-scorecard round of golf. The advantage that the professionals have in this area is their ability to recover from wayward shots. However, even the best of professionals cannot recover from a drive which goes out of bounds, into water or gets lost somewhere. And of course it is always embarrassing to hit an onlooker, although not totally a detriment to your score as it may save you from going out of bounds.

Correct this not-uncommon miscue by paying attention to Figure 11 and taking the appropriate action as dictated by the instruction and the picture. Have confidence, remembering that even the professionals make these mistakes, and while it may result in them not playing on the weekend, it will never prevent you from getting out there whatever day of the week it happens to be.

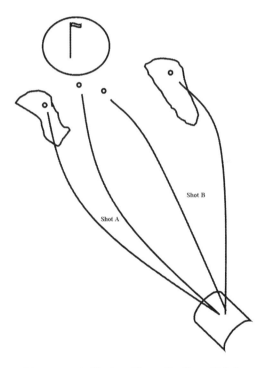

Shot B

Shot A

Figure 11: Drive Goes Left or Right

Figure 11 appears at first to be a complicated situation, but it is not when it is broken down into the two components of Shots A and B. The Shot A on the left ends up in the bunker. If the golfer had aimed 15 to 20 yards more to the right, the ball would be nicely in play just off the green where a chip shot could be used to put the ball in the hole. Similarly, with Shot B, the outermost shot is in the bunker to the right of the hole. Aiming 20 yards more to the left would have prevented the need for a bunker shot. The use of "less" club could have also made sure that the ball did not reach the fairway hazard.

In the situation diagrammed, the fairway is wide enough to allow bunkers (or possibly water) and the ball is not OB (out of bounds) which would cost stroke and distance and at least a double bogey score.

Other variations of this same Figure 11 are possible. While the diagram shows a fade in Shot A and a draw in Shot B, similar outcomes could occur even if the shots were all straight or had the opposite draw or fade.

The reality and the best shot is to hit the ball so that it lands safely in play. Always remember that the centre of the fairway is your friend.

The Driver Super Hint

Look down the fairway, chose a target, whisper to yourself "you're the man," and let it go straight down the middle.

If the fairway has a dogleg within range, put the driver away. Ditto for Par 3's.

Please see Appendix C for the Driving Tracker which is designed to track your drives over five games and allow you to determine your common tendencies. Knowing these tendencies will allow you to concentrate your efforts on the areas identified as problems.

Chapter Four:

Long Irons

I am going to keep this very simple for you so that you can fully understand how to save strokes with long irons. To make this point, I go directly to the Super Hint because this needs no illustration.

Long Iron Super Hint

Never take a long iron out of your bag. Leave them there or better, leave them at home. Use fairway woods and hybrids instead. Get it? Leave them at home. Use them to stake your tomatoes instead. Tell your friends they are getting re-gripped or that you are having someone look at the shafts for possible replacement. DO NOT attempt to play with the long irons!

Chapter Five:

Short Irons

By the time you pull a short iron out of the bag, that is a 7, 8, or 9 iron, you have navigated somehow to within 150 yards of the green. You may have navigated your way to this point with one stroke of the ball (good for you) or with five strokes (silly sandtraps). You are too far away to chip and too close to use a fairway wood. Hence, the short iron is the club of choice.

Generally these are the kindest, most consistent clubs in the bag unless you have a really hot putter. However, it is golf after all and even with these clubs, there can be problems. Let's solve those problems now.

If you are 120 yards from the flag stick and hit a nice shot with your 9 iron, and it does not reach the green as per Figure 12, the solution follows the diagram.

Figure 12: Short Iron is Too Short

The shot in Figure 12 was hit well, but was still too short. You probably think I am going to suggest hitting it harder, but that would be poor advice in this case. Given that the shot was hit well, the correction is to use a lower number club. Yes, I know, that means you have to know how far you hit each of your short irons. Knowledge of club distance is essential. So, get to the driving range and figure that out by hitting each short iron with a ½ swing, a ¾ swing and a full swing and keep track of how far each ball travels.

Here is another bit of good advice. Be very aware of any large rocks between yourself and the putting surface. Local legend has it that golf balls have been known, on occasion, to fly directly backwards from massive rocks, striking the golfer with well-aimed precision, in a part of the body which is extremely sensitive to projectiles of any kind.

The next time you are on the course, use the correct club and hit the ball to the hole as illustrated in Figure 13.

Figure 13: Short Iron Hit Properly

The correct club used properly will give consistent distances. Then all you need to worry about is wind, temperature, uphill/downhill, rain and other possible hindrances to a perfect golf shot such as playing partners who insist on discussing how well they are playing.

Obviously, there can be other problems with the short irons. They can be hit left or right of the green, a little wayward one might say. The correction is the same as was demonstrated in the putting chapter. If you find the shot was too far left, aim more to the right. If too far to the right, aim more to the left. Hit the ball to where you want it to land. Remember, we prefer to hit onto the green rather than close to the green where we are left with a chip shot (unless you are playing a crazy game called "putts" where you can lose money because you land on the green and two-putt instead of landing "safely" off the green and chipping once and then making one putt).

The Short Iron Super Hint

Know how far you hit each short iron when you hit it properly. More simply put, get in the zone and let it rip.

Chapter Six:

Bunker Problems

Sandtraps pose no problem for the professional golfer. Often they see sand as an opportunity to get the ball close to the hole. They would rather have a slightly wayward shot enter the sand than bounce out of bounds or into deep rough or other hazard (see water problems next).

For the regular amateur golfer, sand does pose a problem and there is nothing more frustrating than taking a mighty swing at a ball in the sand and seeing one of two things happen. The first is the sand wedge hitting the ball at the equator and sending is out of the sand trap low and fast, and into another sand trap on the opposite side of the green. The second is seeing an incredible blast of sand and then, when the cloud clears, the gut wrenching disappointment of observing the ball dribble back down to come to rest in the same spot.

These type of shots can make a golfer rather angry, sometimes to the point of doing damage to a club. Did you know it was possible to shake a club to death? Take a deep breath, relax. Really, you are not good enough to warrant anger at a golf shot. Really.

Hit short of the bunker or far enough to clear and avoid the sand trap. If you end up in the sand despite this sage advice, take a deep breath and let it out, take another and swing through the ball hitting the sand behind it and letting the sand lift the ball up and clear of the trap. Repeat as necessary.

The Bunker Super Hint

Unless you are a professional golfer, the bunker is not your friend. You can best save strokes by staying on the green grass.

Chapter Seven:

Water

Golf course designers do not believe in easy courses. They prefer . . . . . challenges . . . . . for the golfers who play on their courses. Some may think that they are in cahoots with the golf ball industry. What an incredible recycling machine is the water hazard! Deep enough to take balls and hide them even from those golfers who have purchased the extending golf ball retriever pole, which is sometimes not quite long enough. Not deep enough that the balls cannot be retrieved with proper equipment. The ball will lie in the water smiling at you.

Water hazards are placed to take the maximum number of golf balls from golfers who make even the slightest error. Furthermore, the rules are such that a golf ball which enters the water can be replaced only by a ball no closer to the hole. In other words, the water is still in play for the next shot allowing the already nervous ball striker an opportunity to lose a second ball.

Cruel course designers will also take advantage of meandering streams which crisscross the fairways bringing repeated misery to the unfortunate.

While it is possible to strike a ball which is in shallow water, it is a risky proposition. Extreme caution and a change of clothing are advised. Figure 14 shows proper procedure if your ball has a proclivity to enter the water.

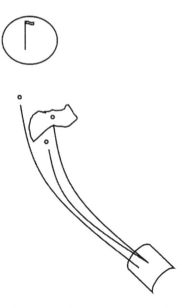

Figure 14: Water Hazard

In Figure 14, the water hazard guards the front of the green and is usually placed at a distance which is in a landing zone which will capture the unwary golfer's ball. If your ball enters the water, as soon as it enters, with or without the benefit of your friends' advice, you are aware that you could have done two things differently and you would be right.

Either you needed to use less club and lay up in front of the water, aiming to the side if possible, or use enough club to go over the hazard. If the correct club had been chosen, you needed to strike it more effectively. Make the decision before you hit the shot knowing your strengths and then smoothly execute one of the options which takes the water out of the equation.

Water Hazard Super Hint

Chose a shot that avoids the water and execute the shot. If all fails, take your lumps, drop a new ball, ignore the cutting comments of your partners and get it over the water.

Chapter Eight:

Mental Part of the Game

Golf is supposed to be a relaxing sport. On a nice day, you walk in a park-like setting or drive a nice cart at a scenic location, hitting and then chasing a small white ball. Can it actually be true that players can win over a million dollars in four days hitting a small white ball into a 4.25 inch hole? Really, it is absurd when one thinks about it rationally

Well, no more absurd than paying eight million dollars to players to chase a piece of frozen rubber along an ice surface or a piece of pigskin up a grass field or knock a ball back and forth across a net or throw a ball past a person holding a wooden bat. We truly have trouble with our priorities some times.

Nevertheless, if one wishes to successfully hit a small white ball with a metal stick along a grassy fairway until it comes to rest at the bottom of a 4.25 inch wide hole in the middle of a well-trimmed lawn, one will hit it better if in control of the mental part of the game.

Tension is the enemy of an effective golf swing. An accelerating, relaxed swing through the golf ball will outperform the tight rigidity of a swing begun at a moment of stress while worried about the water on the left, sand trap ahead, out-of-bounds on the right, rough near the green, and the fact that you just tripled the previous hole.

Hence the mental part of the game is important as a means of lowering the score on the card.

Here are some pointers on overcoming the mental difficulties of the game:

- If you find yourself thinking about the water on the right hand side of the fairway, think about the centre of the landing zone.

- If you find your hands and fingers tight around the grip of the club, loosen them.

- If you are letting your back swing start too quickly, slow it down.

- If you are so tense that you are trying to steer the ball, make a smooth swing and let the ball get in the way.

- If you are being distracted by a sand trap on the left side of the green, ignore it.

- If you are facing a putt and you have a bet on the line and you are nervous about your putt, get over it because if you miss you lose anyway and if you didn't have the money to lose in the first place, you deserve your fate.

- If there is an audience watching your first drive off the tee, learn to disregard them.

- If you are worried about hitting a large rock ahead on the fairway, aim for it so that the odds are that you will miss it.

- Ditto for a tree in the fairway.

- In sum, today's game will not matter when you are 90 so get over it and forget it, besides, it could always have been worse.

Chapter Nine:

Saying the Right Thing

Most games are played in groups. Sometimes the pro shop assigns you friends and sometimes you golf with your regular group. Chit chat is not unusual and invariably there are comments of some sort after each shot.

For a well-hit ball, it is easy to make a comment: great shot, nice hit, incredible!, perfect, etc. All these comments build confidence leading to a better score.

Some people have a knack for saying something positive regardless of the outcome of the shot and some people . . . . do not have that knack. The cruel comment does nothing positive for your game. In fact, the opposite is true. The cruel comment just creates stress which in turn destroys the ability to execute a relaxed swing and enjoy the advantage of a lower score.

In any event, if you observe a bad shot, here is a list of kind things to say and things to avoid as they may be taken as quite nasty and hurtful (unless you don't like your assigned friend and wish to discourage another round).

In all cases, when a ball is hit poorly, never underestimate the value of silence!

You may wish to use the two lists which follow to evaluate the value of your current friends to your game.

Kind things to say after a bad shot

"Too bad"
"Close"
"Good contact"
"A bit left"
"A bit right"
"Almost there"
"We'll find that"
"Sounded good"
"Good read, tough luck"
"It's in play"
"Better luck next time"

"Good line"

"Tough luck"

"Functional miss"

"Well, at least you are on the dance floor"

Cruel things to say after a bad shot:

"Great shot if you don't care where it's going"

"That'll cost you"

"That will be in the water"

"That's four"

"It's headed into the sand"

"That'll find the hazard"

"It's long gone"

"Not your best attempt"

"You didn't catch all of it"

"It's definitely OB"

"No hope for that one"

"Nothing that an operation and 6 weeks in the hospital won't cure"

"Looked like you were trying to kill a snake in a phone booth"

"That almost ended up behind you"

"No need to even look for that one"

"Almost to the ladies' tee"

After a bad putt:

"Nice weight, (sarcastic)
"I thought you had that"
"Nice putt if you don't care about weight or line"
"You are still away"

Sigh, so hurtful. To improve your score you may need to find new friends. However, you may also find that you are saying these things to yourself. If so, find a mirror, look into it, and tell yourself to smarten up.

Chapter Ten:

How to Never Lose a Golf Ball

We started this book with comments about losing golf balls and there is no easier way to achieve a high score than having a ball disappear. Hitting 3 or 5 or 7 off the tee creates a balloon-like effect on the final score of the round.

Golf courses are meant to test. Out of bounds left and right off a tight fairway or insidious water hazards will gobble up the golf balls (which you can retrieve from a used ball store a few weeks later) and have you writing double digits in a tiny box on the score card.

And never think it is just you; it happens on the professional tours too. However, on the tour, you will seldom see it as the suffering players rarely play on the weekend as they tend to miss the cut if they are having these types of rounds.

Alas, there is one and only one true way to avoid these high scores. The clubs have to go. Garage sale, gift to a family member, donation to an aspiring younger player, pro shop used club sale, a ritualistic breaking of the clubs, a satisfying wrapping of each club around a strong tree, or drowning in the water hazard that has done the most damage all are satisfying methods of disposal.

In lieu of the time spent on golf, there will then be an opportunity to take up one of many new endeavours. Fishing comes to mind as does boating, woodworking, landscaping, painting, taking a course, weaving, glass blowing, reading, travelling, home renovations, walking, visiting the relatives more often, washing and waxing the car, tennis, bowling (harder to lose a ball), doing the garage sale tours, gourmet cooking, or making golf clubs (light snicker).

Unfortunately, none of these new activities allows that wonderful feeling when a 40 foot putt turns and drops into the hole or the well-crushed tee shot soars 250 yards straight down the fairway towards the hole.

Argghh, you can't stop playing golf! Go get those clubs back, and my apologies if you used one of the abandonment methods which resulted in their destruction. New clubs are always appropriate. After all, you should not take the blame for shots missed by those old clubs. New ones may solve the problem.

Now get back out there; the course is calling. It wants your golf balls. It craves them. It needs them. Use Appendix E to track your problem areas on the course so you have a record and can avoid the problem the next time you golf that hole. And, if winning is really that important to you, make sure you play with high handicappers.

Chapter Eleven:

Putting it all Together

By now you should recognize the obvious. It's a game, any way you slice it. If it is a game you play for a living, then take it seriously and practice religiously with a teacher who understands your swing and learning style.

If you do not play golf for a living, then don't sweat the small stuff as it won't matter when you are 90. Just play the game. Just play and enjoy. Otherwise Mark Twain was right when he called golf a "good walk spoiled."

Have fun and remember, if your putt is short . . . . next time hit it harder.

Appendix A:

Putting Tracker

Instructions: Keep track of your first putts for five rounds using this easy tracker. Simply tear out and use on the course. Buy another copy of the book if you need to repeat the exercise ☺

Using a check mark, enter the result of your First Putt on each hole (let's assume you will sink the second, or third one, for sure). Total the number of checks at the bottom after your round of golf.

Putting Tracker

Round One: Date:

Hole	Short	Long	Left	Right	Perfect
1					
2					
3					
4					
5					
6					
7					
8					
9					
10					
11					
12					
13					
14					
15					
16					
17					
18					
Total					

Is the "Perfect" column left out and lonely?

Putting Tracker

Round Two: Date:

Hole	Short	Long	Left	Right	Perfect
1					
2					
3					
4					
5					
6					
7					
8					
9					
10					
11					
12					
13					
14					
15					
16					
17					
18					
Total					

See any patterns emerging yet? Make any required adjustments following the tips in Chapter One.

Putting Tracker

Round Three: Date:

Hole	Short	Long	Left	Right	Perfect
1					
2					
3					
4					
5					
6					
7					
8					
9					
10					
11					
12					
13					
14					
15					
16					
17					
18					
Total					

See any improvement yet? The pattern should be clear by now.

Putting Tracker

Round Four: Date:

Hole	Short	Long	Left	Right	Perfect
1					
2					
3					
4					
5					
6					
7					
8					
9					
10					
11					
12					
13					
14					
15					
16					
17					
18					
Total					

One more round to track after this one. If check marks are still in the same columns, review the Putting Super Hint clearly outlined in Chapter 1.

Putting Tracker

Round Five: Date:

Hole	Short	Long	Left	Right	Perfect
1					
2					
3					
4					
5					
6					
7					
8					
9					
10					
11					
12					
13					
14					
15					
16					
17					
18					
Total					

Think positively and consistently follow the tips given. Implementation is crucial. You know what to do now.

Appendix B:

Chipping Tracker

Instructions: Keep track of your chip shots for five rounds using this easy tracker. Simply tear out and use on the course. Buy another copy of the book if you need to repeat the exercise ☺

Using a check mark, enter the result of each chip on each hole (let's assume you will only have one chip per hole, but there are a couple of extra spots just in case). Total the number of checks at the bottom after each round of golf.

Chipping Tracker

Round 1   Date:

Chip	Short	Long	Left	Right	Perfect
1					
2					
3					
4					
5					
6					
7					
8					
9					
10					
11					
12					
13					
14					
15					
16					
17					
18					
19					
20					
Total					

Did you fill it out correctly?

Chipping Tracker

Round 2   Date:

Chip	Short	Long	Left	Right	Perfect
1					
2					
3					
4					
5					
6					
7					
8					
9					
10					
11					
12					
13					
14					
15					
16					
17					
18					
19					
20					
Total					

Any tendencies showing up after two rounds?

Chipping Tracker

Round 3   Date:

Chip	Short	Long	Left	Right	Perfect
1					
2					
3					
4					
5					
6					
7					
8					
9					
10					
11					
12					
13					
14					
15					
16					
17					
18					
19					
20					
Total					

Pattern should be evident by now, or are they all perfect shots?

Chipping Tracker

Round 4   Date:

Chip	Short	Long	Left	Right	Perfect
1					
2					
3					
4					
5					
6					
7					
8					
9					
10					
11					
12					
13					
14					
15					
16					
17					
18					
19					
20					
Total					

Improvement coming into this part of the game?

Chipping Tracker

Round 5   Date:

Chip	Short	Long	Left	Right	Perfect
1					
2					
3					
4					
5					
6					
7					
8					
9					
10					
11					
12					
13					
14					
15					
16					
17					
18					
19					
20					
Total					

Hope you are using less than 20 shots.

Appendix C:

Driving Tracker

Instructions: Keep track of your drives for five rounds using this easy tracker. Simply tear out and use on the course. Buy another copy of the book if you need to repeat the exercise ☺

Using a check mark, enter the result of your drive on each hole. Most regular courses have 14 holes that are Par 4 or Par 5 where you may play the driver if the fairway is straight (and hopefully wide enough). Total the number of checks at the bottom after your round of golf.

Driving Tracker

Round 1   Date:

Hole	Left	Right	Big Dud	Perfect
1				
2				
3				
4				
5				
6				
7				
8				
9				
10				
11				
12				
13				
14				
Total				

Get it filled in okay?

Driving Tracker

Round 2 Date:

Hole	Left	Right	Big Dud	Perfect
1				
2				
3				
4				
5				
6				
7				
8				
9				
10				
11				
12				
13				
14				
Total				

Do you have a few "Perfects" to celebrate?

Driving Tracker

Round 3   Date:

Hole	Left	Right	Big Dud	Perfect
1				
2				
3				
4				
5				
6				
7				
8				
9				
10				
11				
12				
13				
14				
Total				

Starting to see a pattern?

Driving Tracker

Round 4   Date:

Hole	Left	Right	Big Dud	Perfect
1				
2				
3				
4				
5				
6				
7				
8				
9				
10				
11				
12				
13				
14				
Total				

Are they all perfect yet?

Driving Tracker

Round 5   Date:

Hole	Left	Right	Big Dud	Perfect
1				
2				
3				
4				
5				
6				
7				
8				
9				
10				
11				
12				
13				
14				
Total				

Time to make some adjustments. Is putting the driver in a dark, lonely place to punish it an option?

Appendix D:

Complete List of Super-Hints

Chip the ball into the hole from off the green. Never take your putter out of the bag.

Hit the green with your fairway woods. Eliminate the need to chip.

Look down the middle of the fairway and hit the ball straight down the middle.

Never take a long iron out of your bag.

Know how far you hit each short iron when you hit it properly.

Chose a shot that avoids the water and execute the shot.

Save strokes by not entering a bunker.

Don't sweat the small stuff as it won't matter when you are 90

Appendix E:

Personal Record of Things to Remember

Use this page and the next, if necessary to record any stupid things you did during the game which cost you strokes.

Example might be:

Hole 1:

Thought I could clear the water; lay up next time.
It's downhill from the back of the green; hit it lighter.

Etc

Review your list before each round of golf

Stupid mistakes to be avoided at your home course:

More stupid mistakes to avoid on your home course:

Stupid things to avoid on other local courses:

About the Author

Bill Reid is a consultant who is the retired Superintendent of Schools for School District 8 (Kootenay Lake). Born in Scotland, Bill grew up in Ontario where he received an Honours BA in English Literature at Trent University. Other degrees followed over the years including a Bachelor of Education, a Masters Degree in Educational Administration, and a Ph.D. in Educational Leadership.

Bill began teaching in Fort St. John and moved to Nelson to become the principal of L.V. Rogers Secondary School. He has also served the local school district as District Principal for Distance Education, International Programs and Technology, Director of Instruction, and Superintendent of Schools.

Bill consults out of his office in Nelson, British Columbia. He speaks at conferences on a variety of topics such as team building, site-based management, and decision making. He is a certified seminar leader for the True Colors Personality Program.

Bill is the author of <u>101 Nifty Ideas for High Schools</u>, <u>A Baby Boomer's Guide to "I Remember When"</u> and <u>Golf Solved: Simply Doing the Obviously Simple to Improve Your Golf Game</u>.

Bill doesn't like to talk about his handicap (but he does love to golf) ☺

Printed in the United States
By Bookmasters